PRIVATE EYE'S
Colemanballs
2

Another selection of quotes
that originally appeared in
PRIVATE EYE'S 'Colemanballs'
column.
Our thanks once again
to the readers who
sent us their
contributions.

If you enjoyed this book,
the best-selling first

Colemanballs

is still available, as are

Colemanballs 3
Colemanballs 4
Colemanballs 5

D1386982

PRIVATE EYE'S

Colemanballs

2

Compiled and edited by
Barry Fantoni

Illustrated by Larry

PRIVATE EYE

Published in Great Britain 1984
by Private Eye Productions Ltd
6 Carlisle Street, London W1V 5RG

Reprinted 1984 (twice), 1985 (twice), 1986,
1990, 1992, 1994 and 1997

ISBN 1 901784 03 7

Printed in Great Britain by
Cox & Wyman Ltd, Reading, Berkshire

Athletics

. . . some names to look forward to – perhaps in the future.

DAVID COLEMAN

He's 31 this year. Last year he was 30.

DAVID COLEMAN

It's a battle with himself and with the ticking finger of the clock.

DAVID COLEMAN

The late start is due to the time.

DAVID COLEMAN

And with an alphabetical irony Nigeria follows New Zealand.

DAVID COLEMAN

. . . and she finally tastes the sweet smell of success.

IAN EDWARDS

He's running on his nerve-ends.

PETER WEST

Coe has smashed the world record – 1 minute 44.92 seconds has never been run easier.

RON PICKERING

A very powerful set of lungs, very much hidden by that chest of his.

ALAN PASCOE

And the line-up for the final of the Womens' 400 metres hurdles includes three Russians, two East Germans, a Pole, a Swede and a Frenchman.

DAVID COLEMAN

It's obvious these Russian swimmers are determined to do well on American soil.

ANITA LONSBOROUGH

And the mile once again becomes the focal point where it's always been.

RON PICKERING

Boxing

No fighter comes into the ring hoping to win – he goes in hoping to win.

HENRY COOPER

They said it would last two rounds – they were half wrong, it lasted four.

HARRY CARPENTER

Standing there making a sitting target of himself.

TERRY LAWLESS

I'm concentrating so much I don't know what I'm doing myself half the time.

MARK KAYLOR

The Mexicans . . . these tiny little men from South America.

HARRY CARPENTER

And now it comes down to a simple equation – who can stand the heat?

HARRY CARPENTER

The question looming over Magri, is not will he keep the title, but can he?

HARRY CARPENTER

I don't know what impressive is, but Joe was
impressive tonight.

MARLENE BUGNER

It (the fight) has made the richest prize in sport the
richest prize in sport.

JOE BUGNER

. . . and Magri has to do well against this unknown
Mexican who comes from a famous family of five
boxing brothers.

HARRY CARPENTER

I can only see it going one way, that's my way. How
it's actually going to go I can't really say.

NICK WILSHIRE

The Boat Race

. . . and somewhat surprisingly Cambridge have won
the toss.

HARRY CARPENTER

Bowls

(Ken) Strut must be happy to see that ball straggle on and die as short as a carrot.

HARRY RIGBY

Cricket

Anyone foolish enough to predict the outcome of this match is a fool.

FRED TRUEMAN

I don't know if this is his highest score in the John Player League – if not this is his highest score.

ROBERT HUDSON

The first time you face up to a googly you're going to be in trouble if you've never faced one before.

TREVOR BAILEY

It's a truism to say that there's been a change in the weather here at Trent Bridge this morning.

JIM LAKER

He'll certainly want to start by getting off the mark.

DON MOSEY

I was surprised when Geoff Howarth won the toss.

JIM LAKER

People started calling me 'Fiery' because 'Fiery' rhymes with 'Fred' just like 'Typhoon' rhymes with 'Tyson'.

FRED TRUEMAN

Joel Garner – he pockets them for breakfast.

FRED TRUEMAN

So that's 57 runs needed by Hampshire in 11 overs and it doesn't need a calculator to tell us that the run rate required is 5.1818 recurring.

NORMAN DeMESQUITA

That's a remarkable catch by Yardley specially as the ball quite literally rolled along the ground towards him.

MIKE DENNERS

Unless something happens that we can't predict, I
don't think a lot will happen.

FREDDIE TRUEMAN

He caught it like shelling peas.

FRED TRUEMAN

No captain with all the hindsight in the world can
predict how the wicket is going to play.

TREVOR BAILEY

Then there was that dark horse with the golden arm,
Mudassar Nazar.

TREVOR BAILEY

And a sedentary seagull flies by . . .

BRIAN JOHNSTON

And Ian Greig's on eight, including two fours.

JIM LAKER

An interesting morning, full of interest.

JIM LAKER

I think if you've got a safe pair of hands, you've got a safe pair of hands.

TOM GRAVENEY

Cycling

Next week we'll be looking at the Tour de France – all those bicycles roaring through the countryside.

ANDY PEEBLES

Darts

His face is sagging with tension.

SID WADDELL

The fans now, with their eyes pierced on the dart board.

SID WADDELL

He's been burning the midnight oil at both ends.

SID WADDELL

Football

Whoever wins today will win the championship no matter who wins.

DENIS LAW

And Meade had a hat-trick. He scored two goals.

RICHARD WHITMORE

In Scotland football hooliganism has been met by banning alcohol from grounds but in England this solution has been circumnavigated.

WALLACE MERCER

The boys' feet have been up in the clouds since the win.

ALAN BUCKLEY

Chesterfield 1 Chester 1. Another score draw there in the local derby.

DESMOND LYNAM

The dice are stacked against them.

THEO FOLEY

Spurs, one of the in-form teams of the moment with six successive wins are almost as impressive as Queen's Park Rangers with five . . .

BOB WILSON

I'm not superstitious or anything like that, but I'll just hope we'll play our best and put it in the lap of the Gods.

TERRY NEILL

Bryan Robson – well, he does what he does and his
future is in the future.

RON GREENWOOD

The whole team stopped as one man, but Arkwright
in particular.

BRIAN MOORE

Well clearly Graeme it all went according to plan –
what was the plan exactly?

ELTON WELLSBY

Wayne Clarke, one of the famous Clarke family . . .
and he's one of them, of course . . .

BRIAN MOORE

It's a Renaissance – or, put more simply, some you
win, some you lose.

DESMOND LYNAM

I don't blame individuals, Elton, I blame myself.

JOE ROYLE

Football's a game of skill . . . we kicked them a bit and they kicked us a bit.

GRAHAM ROBERTS

Nottingham Forest are having a bad run . . . they've lost six matches now without winning.

DAVID COLEMAN

£5.3 million is a large loaf to be throwing away before a ball's been kicked.

JIMMY GREAVES

Players win games and players lose games – it's all about players really.

BOBBY FERGUSON

His strengths were my weaknesses and my weaknesses were his strengths.

JOHN BOND

There is no change in the top six of Div. II except that Leeds United have moved into the top six.

FRED DINAGE

So that's 1–0, sounds like the score at Bondary Park where of course it's 2–2.

JACK WAINWRIGHT

Kicked wide of the goal with such precision.

DESMOND LYNAM

I do want to play the long ball and I do want to play the short ball. I think long and short balls is what football is all about.

BOBBY ROBSON

INTERVIEWER: In your new book, Pat, you've devoted a whole chapter to Jimmy Greaves.
PAT JENNINGS: Yes that's right . . . well what can you say about Jimmy?

You can see how O'Leary is absolutely racked with pain, and realises it.

BRIAN MOORE

At the end of the day, it's all about what's on the shelf at the end of the year.

STEVE COPPELL

. . . and now the Northern Ireland Manager, Billy Bingham, will have to put his thinking boots on.

RADIO COMMENTATOR, BBC

I am a firm believer that if you score one goal the other team have to score two to win.

HOWARD WILKINSON

So it means that, mathematically, Southampton have 58 points.

PETER JONES

If you had to name one particular person to blame it would have to be the players.

THEO FOLEY

We are really the victims of our own problems.

JIMMY GREAVES

UNOFFICIAL HEIGHT 2' 6"

TRAINER

Here's Brian Flynn. His official height is five feet five
and he doesn't look much taller than that.

ALAN GREEN

Mabut has now played seven consecutive games for
England. This is the seventh.

MARTIN TYLER

I'd have to be superman to do some of the things I'm supposed to have done . . . I've been in six different places at six different times.

GEORGE BEST

That's a question-mark everyone's asking.

BRUCE GROBBELAR

DICKIE DAVIES: What's he going to be telling his team at half-time, Denis?
DENIS LAW: He'll be telling them that there are 45 minutes left to play . . .

Well, as for Ian Rush – he's perfectly fit – apart, that is, from his physical fitness . . .

MIKE ENGLAND

I'm not going to make it a target but it's something to aim for.

STEVE COPPELL

And now International Soccer Special: Manchester Utd v. Southampton.

DAVID COLEMAN

Well Ibrox is filling up slowly, but rapidly.

JAMES SANDERSON

Hodge scored for Forest after only 22 seconds, totally against the run of play.

PETER LORENZO

Queen's Park against Forfar – you can't get more
romantic than that.

ARCHIE McPHERSON

We are quite lucky really this year because Christmas
falls on Christmas day.

BOBBY GOULD

He put it just where he meant it and it passed the
Luxembourg goalpost by 18 inches.

BRYON BUTLER

Ardiles always says 'If you're confident you're always
totally different to the player that's lacking
confidence'.

KEITH BURKINSHAW

The goals made such a difference to the way this game
went.

JOHN MOTSON

Well we got nine and you can't score more than that.

BOBBY ROBSON

This is a tremendous asset for the club, a tremendous
headache lifted off our shoulders, really.

ELTON JOHN

The only thing Norwich didn't get was the goal that
they finally got.

JIMMY GREAVES

We could be putting the hammer in Luton's coffin.

RAY WILKINS

Football's football; if that weren't the case it wouldn't be the game that it is.

GARTH CROOKS

I predicted in August Celtic would reach the final. On the eve of the final I stand by that prediction.

J. SANDERSON

. . . and with 8 minutes left the game could be won or lost in the next 5 or 10 minutes.

JIMMY ARMFIELD

IAN ST JOHN: Is he speaking to you yet?
JIMMY GREAVES: Not yet, but I hope to be
incommunicado with him in a very short space of
time.

It's a game of two teams.

PETER BRACKLEY

Wolves keeper John Burridge has consciously
modelled himself on the great Peter Shilton . . . same
sort of hairstyle.

BRYON BUTLER

If England had scored in the first half, I think the young legs would have found younger hearts inside them.

JIMMY ARMFIELD

Systems are made by players rather than players making systems.

THEO FOLEY

. . . and then there was Johan Cruyff, who at 35 has added a whole new meaning to the word Anno Domini.

ARCHIE McPHERSON

I don't really believe in targets, because my next target is to beat Stoke City.

RON WYLIE

And at the end of the season you can only do as well as what you have done.

BRYAN ROBSON

Real possession football, this. And Zico's lost it.

JOHN HELM

I can't see us getting beat now – once we get our tails
in front.

JIM PLATT

They can crumble as easily as ice cream in this heat.

SAMMY NELSON

Don't tell those coming in now the result of that
fantastic match. Now let's have another look at Italy's
winning goal.

DAVID COLEMAN

A few question marks are being asked in the
Honduran defence.

ALAN GREEN

The acoustics seem to get louder.

HUGH JOHNS

Being given chances – and not taking them. That's
what life's all about.

RON GREENWOOD

And Wilkins sends an inch-perfect pass to no one in particular

BRYON BUTLER

To me personally, it's nothing personal to me.
RON GREENWOOD

It is a cup final and the one that wins it goes through.
JIMMY HILL

He's marked his entrance with an error of some momentum.

BARRY DAVIES

Even when you're dead you shouldn't lie down and
let yourself be buried.

GORDON LEE

. . . but the ball was going all the way, right away,
eventually.

ARCHIE McPHERSON

And Ritchie has now scored 11 goals, exactly double
the number he scored last season.

ALAN PARRY

Quiroga touches it away. Nothing he doesn't do that isn't spectacular.

GERRY HARRISON

Socrates – so named because his father was interested in Greek mythology.

COMMENTATOR, ITV

The Spaniards have been reduced to aiming aimless balls into the box.

RON ATKINSON

On this 101st FA Cup Final day, there are just two teams left.

DAVID COLEMAN

That shot might not have been as good as it might have been.

JOHN MOTSON

And Wigan Athletic are certain to be promoted barring a mathematical tragedy.

TONY GUBBA

Again Mariner and Butcher are trying to work the oracle on the near post.

MARTIN TYLER

He hit that one like an arrow.

ALAN PARRY

Football's all about 90 minutes . . .

GLEN HODDLE

In fact that's Swindon's first win of any kind in nine matches.

DAVID COLEMAN

I felt a lump in my mouth as the ball went in.

TERRY VENABLES

It's always very satisfying to beat Arsenal, as indeed Arsenal would admit.

PETER JONES

John Bond has brought in a young left sided midfield player who, I guess, will play on the left side of midfield.

JIMMY ARMFIELD

BRYON BUTLER: You'd obviously made up your mind to play both Stein and Walsh?
BOBBY ROBSON: Yes – I thought that individually and as a pair, they'd do better together.

And the second goal was a blue-print of the first.

BRYON BUTLER

I'd like to have seen Tony Morley left on as a down
and out winger.

JIMMY ARMFIELD

Most of the people who can remember when we were
a great club are dead.

NOTTS COUNTY FC CHAIRMAN

One of Asa's great qualities is not scoring goals.

ROY SMALL

Whelan was in the position he was, exactly.

JIMMY ARMFIELD

It feels like winning the cup final, if that's what it feels like.

GRAHAM HAWKINS

The last player to score a hat-trick in a cup final was Stan Mortenson. He even had a final named after him – the Matthews final.

LAWRIE McMENEMY

The only thing I have in common with George Best is that we came from the same place, play for the same club and were discovered by the same man.

NORMAN WHITESIDE

Arsenal, with Petrovic anonymous.

DAVID DAVIES

Obviously for Scunthorpe it would be a nice scalp to put Wimbledon on their bottoms.

DAVE BASSETT

Wallace, moving forward, his red hair always in the action.

PETER JONES

The match has become quite unpredictable — but it still looks as though Arsenal will win the cup.

JOHN MOTSON

There was a paradox of air in the town when we arrived in Watford this afternoon.

ANDY SMITH

Great goal by Moss — straight into the textbook.

GERRY HARRISON

If you stand still there is only one way to go, and that's backwards.

PETER SHILTON

Not the first half you might have expected, even though the score might suggest that it was.

JOHN MOTSON

I don't know if that result's enough to lift Birmingham off the bottom of the table, although it'll certainly take them above Sunderland.

MIKE INGHAM

Golf

Pinero has missed the putt – I wonder what he's thinking in Spanish.

RENTON LAIDLAW

He (Jon Bland) certainly didn't appear as cool as he looked . . .

RENTON LAIDLAW

I owe a lot to my parents, especially my mother and my father.

GREG NORMAN

Horses

. . . and in 1900 the owner of the Grand National winner was the then Prince of Wales, King Edward VII.

DAVID COLEMAN

There's Pam (Dunning) watching anxiously. She doesn't look anxious though.

STEPHEN HADLEY

As you travel the world, do you do a lot of travelling?

HARVEY SMITH

He's a very competitive competitor, that's the sort of
competitor he is.

DORIAN WILLIAMS

Ice Skating

Just look at that. Nine 'six' marks, every one of them
a 'six'.

ALAN WEEKS

This speed skating is taking place virtually in the
shadow of the Olympic flame.

RON PICKERING

Motor Racing

Even as I speak, in four hours time the Kyalami
Grand Prix will roar away.

TONY LEWIS

. . . the lead is now 6.9 seconds. In fact it's just under
7 seconds.

MURRAY WALKER

I wonder if Watson is in the relaxed state of mind that
he's in.

MURRAY WALKER

The gap between the two cars is 0.9 of a second –
which is less than one second.

MURRAY WALKER

Tombay's hopes, which were nil before, are
absolutely zero now.

MURRAY WALKER

Your luck goes up and down like swings and
roundabouts.

JAMES HUNT

You can't see a digital clock because there isn't one.
MURRAY WALKER

Oddballs

. . . and the hourglass ticking off the seconds.

WALDEMAR JANUSZCZAK

Attached to the bottom corner is a rope of finite
length.

GORDON BURNS

MICK ANDREWS: He looks small, doesn't he?
PETER PURVES: Well he is small himself.

KICK START

Are you married?
CALLER: No, engaged.
What, engaged to your fiancee?

PETER POWELL

He has waited 62 years to meet the brother he never
knew he had.

BBC NEWS REPORTER

Let's take an example
from both ends of the
social pyramid.
THE WORLD TONIGHT

They say there are 60,000 lakes here in Finland and
there must be twice as many pine trees.
ALAN PARRY

The Sidmouth Festival succeeds in bringing the
corners of the spectrum together.
IAN A. ANDERSON

You went to Miami, to the Kennedy Space Centre.
You were obviously in Florida.

DAVID HAMILTON

Yup, I suppose the cards were on the wall really . . .
PETER POWELL

How priceless are these things?
RUSSELL HARTY

As usual it's 3 minutes past 8 o'clock.
DAVID JENSEN

Looks like being a busy weekend on the ferries,
particularly Saturday and Sunday.
PETER POWELL

It is now 5 past 12, sometime on Sunday night.
TOM BOSWELL

. . . so if you've got a birthday coming up within the
next twelve months or so . . .
LYNDA BERRY

We forced them to see that reason prevails, not force.
JIM SLATER

Has there ever been any link between asbestos and asbestos-linked diseases?

JIMMY YOUNG

We would like to welcome back long wave listeners and apologise for the 20 minute break in transmission. We hope it didn't spoil your enjoyment of Thirty Minute Theatre.

ANNOUNCER, BBC RADIO 4

SIMON BATES: What do you do?
CONTESTANT: I'm a housewife and mother.
SIMON BATES: Got any kids?

Nobody could convince me that they'd still be alive if they hadn't been wearing a seat belt.

DR KEITH LITTLE

It was the most unanimous decision I have seen.

OWEN BRISCOE

Video-discs, one of the next big things, has been a flop.

PAUL GAMBACCINI

As our regular listeners will know, Christmas has come and gone.

DOUGLAS CAMERON

. . . and it's exactly 9 minutes past 9 – and that doesn't happen very often.

DOUGLAS MOFFAT

Clacton Pier Management who have spent two
million pounds in as many years . . .

JOHN BACON

Of course Kirkpatrick will serve nowhere near the
900 years to which he has been sentenced because the
system in Northern Ireland allows for up to 50%
remission for good behaviour.

N. IRISH CORRESPONDENT

In this duet from the 'Barber of Seville', the title role
is sung by Victoria de los Angeles.

RADIO 3

Les Dawson offers his contratulations on the birth of the baby – and after all, he should know. He drove tanks in Korea.

SELINA SCOTT

Many people think that Joan of Arc was immortal but she did in fact exist.

DOUGGIE BROWN

The pip has been squeezed dry . . .

RON KEATING

The British troops are now close enough to Port
Stanley to see Argentinians in their houses eating
their dinner through binoculars.

BRIAN HANRAHAN

This marks the end of a long life and an even longer
career.

PAULINE BUSHNELL

Do you think there's a prolonged water-workers strike in the pipeline?

PAUL LARSMAN

. . . and of course Greg Strange who needs no introduction. He's motoring correspondent for LBC.

CAROL THATCHER

Nuclear war lies, if it lies anywhere, in the future.
LUDOVIC KENNEDY

The time at 8.20 just coming up to 8.20.
DON MOSLEY

Finally, but by no means last . . .
ANDY PEEBLES

That alters the ballpark altogether.
LORD MATTHEWS

The Falklands Crisis has reached a critical stage.
ANDREW MANDERSTAM

Port Stanley airport is surrounded by howitzers
pointing skywards – which is the direction from which
an air attack would most likely come from.
BBC1

When this table was first made it was brand new.
ARTHUR NEGUS

The increase in whisky prices is not as great as expected and with a recession in Scotland 10p is better than nothing.

DEREK COOPER

He has had to put his finger in the dyke in order to prevent any fall-out from this having a boomerang effect.

HEARST NEWSPAPERS REPORTER

We went to see the Sistine Chapel, one of the holiest places in the Christian world, the ceiling all covered in Gods and Goddesses.

DEREK NIMMO

Tell me, what is your gut-feeling in your heart of hearts?

TODAY PROGRAMME

Last time they went out and they got their fingers burnt. What guarantee can you give that they won't catch a cold this time?

INTERVIEWER, 'Today Programme'

What sun there was today could be counted on one hand.

WEATHERMAN

CALLER: I'm 21, Peter.
P.P.: You sound much younger.
CALLER: A lot of people say that.
P.P.: How old are you?

PETER POWELL

You can bet your boots if the shoe was on the other foot the Americans wouldn't wear it.

SANDRA DICKENSON

Butter is just the pawn in the political game of draughts.

TONY DE ANGELI

One should be suspicious of any vehicle which gives rise to suspicion.

COMMANDER JOHN HUCKLESBY

Here's some Spike Milligan. Good Friday should be a bit silly.

DAVE LEE TRAVERS

They speak all the languages of the rainbow there.

JACKIE STEWART

I wanted him to be the kind of man who had never walked along the beach and felt the grass under his feet.

BILL FORSYTH

The Clarks, who have been one of the great Victorian families for centuries.
                    CHRISTOPHER MARTIN JENKINS

And for those who want to deal in metric that's a girth of 22 feet and a height of about 230 feet.
                    DAVID BELLAMY

I turned to see all the onlookers looking on.
                    ANNEKA RICE

I don't think it's any less important for not being terribly important.
                    PATRICK KEIGHLEY

The increase in whisky prices is not as great as expected and with a recession 10p is better than nothing.
                    DEREK COOPER

Peter Powell: So, your son was born on the very day Radio 1 actually started?
Caller: Yes, that's correct. He was born sixteen years ago today.
Peter Powell: How old is your son now?

This one is for Nigel Addison – I went to school with a Nigel Addison, I wonder if it's his brother.

PETER POWELL

I see my mum as much as I like – which is not as often as I'd like.

LEO SAYER

These past five weeks have passed at the drop of a pin.
RACHEL HEYHOE-FLINT

But obviously you do other things as well as
dedicating your lives 24 hours a day to ballet.
MIKE READ

Politics

Those of us who lived through the Falklands Crisis –
and I am one of them . . .
FRANCIS PYM

We were unanimous – in fact everyone was unanimous.

ERIC HEFFER

If I were chairman of the election campaign committee, that somebody would be me.

DAVID STEEL

I don't want to make any previous statement on that.

GEORGE SCHULTZ

For some time now, the Italian government have
been tightening the screws on terrorists from both
ends of the political rainbow.

ALEXANDER MACLEOD

Pop

He wrote such lovely music in his lifetime.

DAVID JACOBS

I've read a lot and heard a lot about (Jim) Morrison,
but I don't know much about him.

JOE ELLIOTT

This is the greatest record of all time for me at the
moment.

STEVE WRIGHT

On Monday we'll have Jerry Lee Lewis, on Tuesday Chuck Berry and on Wednesday Elvis Presley, though not in that order.

KID JENSEN

John Paul Young with his Greatest and only Hit.

CHARLES NOVE

Of course song-writers are the unsung heroes of these days.

KEITH FORDYCE

If there are as many Flintstones fans around as me, this will be a monster hit.

MIKE READ

I don't know if I have heard that before – if so it was on a record I haven't played.

KEN STEWART

I never thought Jeff Beck and myself would ever play together, but I was there the night it happened.

JIMMY PAGE

Spice is the variety of life.

JIMMY SAVILE

And you can't get much further outside the Top
Ten than number eleven.

JIMMY SAVILE

Ian Gillan. A lot of people think his image is not right, but they'd be on their own.

MIKE QUINN

And there was Donovan, reigning supreme at number eight.

ALAN FREEMAN

It was like the Sixties, but it wasn't the Sixties – it was 1969.

JIMMY SAVILE

Stuart Sutcliffe left the Beatles when he died.

PHILIP NORMAN

I never ever knew where Rome was. That's how good I was at History.

RICK PARFITT

I like the kind of pop that's here today and gone tomorrow and you can hear it ten years later and think, that's fantastic!

ROGER DALTRY

Do you like their records, or is it just the music you go for?

SIMON BATES

. . . in those days, number two was, in a funny sort of way, also number one.

JIMMY SAVILE

It's all Beatles music from noon until midday.

MIKE SMITH

It's taken two years for that to be a hit. It's straight in at 35.

SIMON BATES

I'll make no comment on that, because it's the first time I've heard it — but it just sounds great.

PETER POWELL

I spoke to Boy George between four and four-thirty some time today.

PETER POWELL

They're a six man vocal singing group.

PETER POWELL

No-one knew how long that rock and roll explosion was going to last, if you look back in retrospect.

ALAN PRICE

And you can't get nearer the top ten than number twelve.

JIMMY SAVILE

I'm sure this will evoke memories for everyone, even those of us who don't remember it.

MARK ELLEN

You can't get much further outside the top ten than this — at number 11, it's Atomic Rooster.

JIMMY SAVILE

Ron White was not one of the very first original members of the Motown staff, but eventually he was.

SMOKEY ROBINSON

Their stage act was one of the highlights of their live performances.

ANNE NIGHTINGALE

Red Red Wine by UB40 – Number 1 in the charts and doing even better in Europe.

BILLY BUTLER

I'm not even going to ignore that.

LYNSEY DE PAUL

The best track on that album isn't on it.

PETER YOUNG

Aren't you concerned that as the great rock and roll machine takes more and more a part of your life, that your roots will slide under the door?

ANDY PEEBLES

It comes from a film called 'An Officer and a Gentleman', and it's the title song – 'Up Where We Belong'.

MIKE SMITH

This is their first single, and their most successful so far.

MARK CURRY

Rugby

And there's Kenney, who at times looks almost like his double.

NIGEL STARMER-SMITH

If you didn't know him, you wouldn't know who he was.

NIGEL STARMER-SMITH

. . . and Dusty Hare kicked 19 of the 17 points.

DAVID COLEMAN

Of course they don't play to any sort of pattern and if you're not careful you will start playing to that pattern.

MIKE DAVIS

An easy kick for George Fairburn now but, as everybody knows, no kicks are easy.

DAVID DOYLE-DAVIDSON

Snooker

Ninety-nine times out of a thousand he would have potted that ball.

TED LOWE

This match has gradually and suddenly come to a climax.

DAVID VINE

He's lucky in one sense and lucky in the other.

TED LOWE

Oh and that's a brilliant shot. The odd thing is his mum's not very keen on snooker.

TED LOWE

Higgins first entered the Championship ten years ago; that was for the first time, of course.

TED LOWE

Just enough points here for Tony to pull the cat out of the fire.

RAY EDMONDS

And it is my guess that Steve Davis will try to score as many points as he can in this frame.

TED LOWE

Tony Meo beginning to find his potting boots . . .
REX WILLIAMS

Suddenly Alex Higgins was 7–0 down.
DAVID VINE

When you start off it's nil-nil.

STEVE DAVIS

Steve Davis has a tough consignment in front of him.
TED LOWE

From this position you've got to fancy either your opponent or yourself winning.
KIRK STEVENS

A little pale in the face, but then his name is White.
TED LOWE

This said, the inevitable failed to happen.
JOHN PULMAN

No-one came closer to winning the World Title last year than the runner-up Dennis Taylor.
DAVID VINE

That pot puts the game beyond reproach.
TED LOWE

He'll have no trouble in solving the solution.
JACK KARNEHAM

I've always said the difference between winning and losing is nothing at all.

TERRY GRIFFITHS

Well, valour was the better part of discretion there.

JACK KARNEHAM

Sometimes the deciding frame's always the toughest to win.

DENNIS TAYLOR

All square all the way round.

TED LOWE

There is, I believe, a time limit for playing a shot. But I think it's true to say that nobody knows what that limit is.

TED LOWE

Ray Reardon, one of the great Crucible champions — won it five times, when the championship was played away from the Crucible.

DAVID VINE

Jimmy White has that wonderful gift of being able to point his cue where his is looking.

TED LOWE

10–4 . . . and it could mean exactly what that means.

DAVID VINE

And now snooker. And Steve Davis has crashed out of the U.K. Billiards Championship.

ALLAN TAYLOR

Tennis

He's got his hands on his knees and holds his head in despair.

PETER JONES

The Gullikson twins here. An interesting pair – both from Wisconsin.

DAN MASKELL

These ball boys are marvellous. You don't even notice them. There's a left-handed one over there. I noticed him earlier.

MAX ROBERTSON

. . . and when Chrissie is playing well I always feel that she is playing well.

ANNE JONES

It's quite clear that Virginia Wade is thriving on the pressure now that the pressure on her to do well is off.

HARRY CARPENTER

When Martina is tense it helps her relax.

DAN MASKELL

We haven't had any more rain since it stopped raining.

HARRY CARPENTER

Lendl has remained throughout as calm as the proverbial iceberg.

DAN MASKELL

Billie Jean King, with the look on her face that says she can't believe it . . . because she never believes it, and yet, somehow, I think she does.

MAX ROBERTSON

You can almost hear the silence as they battle it out.

DAN MASKELL

This is the third week the fish seem to be getting away from British tennis players.

GERALD WILLIAMS

Strawberries, cream and champers flowed like hot cakes.

BBC RADIO 2

She comes from a tennis playing family. Her father's a Dentist.

BBC TENNIS COMMENTATOR